Original title:
Shrubbery Songs

Copyright © 2025 Creative Arts Management OÜ
All rights reserved.

Author: Isaac Ravenscroft
ISBN HARDBACK: 978-1-80566-636-3
ISBN PAPERBACK: 978-1-80566-921-0

The Melody of Leaves

The leaves do dance with whispered glee,
As squirrels sing their harmony.
With branches swaying side to side,
The forest joins in this playful ride.

A buzzing bee plays trumpet loud,
While crickets chirp, a merry crowd.
The trees, they laugh, in rustles bright,
As sunlight spills its golden light.

Echoes of Underbrush

In tangled knots where shadows blend,
The fox and hedgehog shake a friend.
They organize a prank, so sly,
While butterflies swirl in the sky.

The underbrush has jokes to share,
With buzzing bugs all everywhere.
A rabbit jumps, a stick does crack,
Creating laughter in the back.

Ballads of the Ferns

The ferns stand proud, in sunlight's beam,
With stories hidden in their green seam.
Their whispers weave a silly tale,
Of gnomes who wear their hats like sail.

A lazy lizard strums a song,
While twigs and leaves all sing along.
The breezy air brings forth a cheer,
As woodland critters gather near.

Serenades at Dusk

As dusk unfolds its velvet cape,
The fireflies dance in tiny shape.
A toad croaks notes, high and low,
While puppeting the shadows' show.

The moonlight chuckles on the ground,
With footloose critters all around.
In this soft glow, they spin and twirl,
Creating tunes that make hearts whirl.

A Balance of Blooms

In a garden where gnomes play,
The daisies dance in bright array.
A squirrel juggles acorn pies,
While gossip flies between the flies.

Bees wearing hats buzz with flair,
Chasing butterflies through the air.
There's laughter under leafy caps,
As nature joins in silly laps.

The Peace of the Perennial

The daisies wear a peaceful crown,
While dandelions tumble down.
A peace treaty signed by a tree,
Says, 'No weeds allowed, just let it be!'

A ladybug prances with zest,
Declaring the garden's a guest.
The tulips giggle, swaying wide,
While ants serve tea on the side.

Echoing in Enclave

In the enclave where laughter brews,
A hedgehog tickles with his shoes.
The ferns whisper jokes to the wind,
While snails judge the race—who will win?

The lilacs chuckle at the sun,
As shadows dance and have their fun.
With every rustle, a joke unfolds,
In the laughter of blossoms, life beholds.

The Story of the Shrubland

Once upon a time in the green,
A raccoon wore pants, so serene.
The shrubs all gathered 'round to see,
A tale told by a wise old bee.

'In this land of giggles and cheer,
We grow so wild without a fear.
A dance-off starts under the moon,
As flowers hum a playful tune.'

Lush Lyrics of the Lawn

In the grass, an ant's parade,
With tiny hats, they're not afraid.
They side-step weeds, a wobbly dance,
Giving each other a silly glance.

A daisy's grin, so white and bright,
Tickles the toes of a worm in flight.
While buzzing bees hum a jolly tune,
Around a toadstool, they laugh at the moon.

The Harmony of Honeysuckle

Honeysuckle whispers sweet and low,
Singing to petals as breezes blow.
A bumblebee snacks, with a slurpy sound,
On nectar treats that are all around.

A ladybug dons her polka-dot dress,
And twirls with glee in the floral mess.
Grasshoppers join in a hopping show,
As the sun dips down, putting on a glow.

Tinkling Tunes in the Thorns

Thorns play tricks in the prickle band,
Tickling noses, oh isn't it grand!
A hedgehog laughs, rolling on the ground,
While sparrows chirp their merry sound.

The roses blush, their petals sway,
As cats chase shadows that dart and play.
With whispers of joy, the garden hums,
Nature's giggles, oh how it comes!

The Inspired Blooms

Petunias paint in colors bright,
While chubby bunnies hop with delight.
In the soft breeze, each flower sways,
As garden gnomes chuckle through sunny days.

The sunflowers stretch, wearing their crowns,
While ants hold meetings in mini towns.
With blooming laughter and scents galore,
In this happy patch, who could ask for more?

Verses of the Vine

Have you seen the vine in dance?
It sways to the music, ready to prance.
With leaves that giggle, they tickle the air,
Nature's own jester, without a care.

In the garden, it tells a tale,
Of worms on vacation, and snails on sale.
A party of colors, quite the delight,
An invite to all, both day and night.

Cadence of the Canes

The canes gather round with a whispering sound,
In a merry old circle, where laughter's profound.
With twigs as their legs, they shake and sway,
A dance of the bushes, in bright spring rays.

They gossip of bugs with a cheeky grin,
And secrets of roots with a roguish spin.
In shadows they flutter and stay out of sight,
Plotting their mischief from dawn until night.

The Introduction of Ivy

Oh ivy, oh ivy, you cling with such flair,
Your humorous twirls make the walls seem debonair.
With a wink and a nod, you climb with a cheer,
The true comedian of the year!

Around every corner, you peek and you pry,
Inviting the bees for a small cup of chai.
Your leaves tell a joke, in their verdant disguise,
While the sun shines bright, you humor the skies.

Aria of the Arbors

Under arches of green, the trees have a ball,
Singing in whispers, their melodies call.
With branches that wiggle and roots that jest,
The whole forest hums, it's a merry fest.

They boast of the rain and the sun's warm embrace,
Each rustle a laugh, in this lively place.
A concert of leaves with the wind as the guest,
Together they play in nature's own quest.

Harmonies in the Underbrush

In the thicket, whispers hum,
Bugs and birds in tune, they strum.
A squirrel dances with great pride,
  Tripping over roots that hide.

Laughter from the leafy crowns,
Frogs in chorus, hopping clowns.
A bunny drumming with its feet,
  Creating quite the funky beat.

The Rustling Choir

Windswept branches sway and creak,
The rustling leaves begin to speak.
A raccoon sings a witty song,
Echoes bounce, they can't be wrong.

The fox joins in, its voice so sly,
As crickets play the night nearby.
The chorus grows, a merry mix,
Nature's band cannot be fixed.

Rhythms of the Shaded Grove

Underneath the leafy shade,
Critters dance in wild parade.
A chipmunk jigs, with sparkly eyes,
While owls hoot in foolish guise.

They stomp and sway, a joyful sight,
As fireflies twinkle in the night.
Each creature brings a playful flair,
Grooves from nature's rhythmic air.

Melodies from the Woodland Edge

At twilight's hour, the songs take flight,
From every nook, a pure delight.
The woodpecker knocks a silly beat,
As hedgehogs sway with tiny feet.

Through tangled paths, the laughter flows,
With jokes that only nature knows.
Each note a chuckle, every tune,
Bringing smiles beneath the moon.

Love Letters in the Thicket

In tangled vines, a note concealed,
A squirrel finds it, giggling, revealed.
With acorn ink, he scribbles away,
His love for the nut, brightening the day.

A dandelion sways, a sweet serenade,
To a passing bee, his charm on parade.
Blushing petals, they flutter and preen,
In the court of the wild, a romantic scene.

The Nature's Whisk of Embrace

A gentle breeze, a tickling tease,
As leaves exchange secrets with playful ease.
A branch does a jig, oh, what a sight,
While bushes giggle under the moonlight.

Here comes the mist, with a whirling spin,
Tickling the flowers, they'll laugh till they grin.
Nature's own prankster, in branches entwined,
A ludicrous waltz, hilariously designed.

Whispers Among the Green

In the green expanse, where giggles collide,
Each rustling leaf, a secret to confide.
A bashful fern blushes, hiding its face,
While daisies gossip, keeping up the pace.

The hedgehog chuckles, rolling with glee,
As critters convene for a lively tee-hee.
With nature's own humor, they share in the cheer,
In whispers among greens, laughter draws near.

Harmonies in the Thicket

A jazzed-up robin sings loud from a bough,
With rhythm from nature, as odd as a cow.
The crickets join in, a curious band,
In a thicket of fun, they take a stand.

A violin spider spins melodies grand,
While beetles provide beats, all well planned.
In this woodland theater, they dance and they play,
With harmonies bubbling, in nature's ballet.

Open Mic in the Orchard

Under the apple tree's grin,
A worm croons, it's quite the win.
Grasshoppers tap their feet with glee,
As squirrels decide who will be free.

Cherries sway to the silly beat,
While bees buzz, they can't feel defeat.
A raccoon strums a leaf guitar,
He dreams of being a rock star!

Peaches throw little parties all night,
Wobbling softly in the moonlight.
Loud laughter from branches above,
An orchard stage, a fruit-filled love.

With every pluck and every cheer,
The fruit folks gather and draw near.
Come join the fun, don't be shy!
The trees are singing, oh my my!

Whims of the Willows

In the breeze, the willows sway,
Their long arms dance, come what may.
A rabbit hops, a grin on its face,
As branches tickle at a lively pace.

Frogs leap in and out of the reeds,
Singing songs of funny deeds.
Old turtle tells tales that make us laugh,
While fireflies shine their quirky path.

Bouncing bugs hold a conference grand,
Debating who has the comfiest land.
The whispering leaves giggle away,
Oh, the secrets they share every day!

With willow whispers, the laughter flows,
Nature's humor, it giggles and glows.
Join the whimsy, don't miss the show,
For every blossom has tales to sow!

A Tapestry of Tangles

Tangled vines in a knotty mess,
Dancing twirls in their leafy dress.
A chubby squirrel lost his way,
In a dilemma, he starts to play.

Mice run around, without a care,
Bumping into flowers, unaware.
Petals giggle, their colors bright,
As they watch the scurry in delight.

Brambles laugh, teasing shy young leaves,
While ladybugs share their silly thieves.
A webbed magician shows his tricks,
With these creatures, the humor sticks!

Each twist and turn breaks out in song,
Nature's chaos where all belong.
In this tapestry of giggles, we find,
A world untangled, oh so kind!

The Brushstroke of Botany

In the garden so lush, the weeds start to dance,
With a jig and a wiggle, they take their chance.
The daisies declare, "We're the flowers supreme!"
While the dandelions giggle, "We're just part of the dream!"

The rose, with a pout, said, "Why don't you glow?"
The thistle replied, "It's just part of the show!"
But all the wild blooms, despite their loud prattle,
Know they're all jesters in nature's great battle.

Lyrical Landscapes

The tulips are singing in a colorful choir,
While the violets whisper, sharing their fire.
A squirrel joins in with a tap on the ground,
As sunlight spills laughter, the best kind of sound.

Here come the odd herbs, with a quirky old tune,
Their parsley prances under the light of the moon.
With each silly leaf, the garden will sway,
Rhythm and roots make a fabulous play!

Chords of the Creeping Mustard

Upon the lawn, mustard takes center stage,
With a tune so bold, it breaks through the cage.
Chickweed sings backup in a costume of green,
While the bold buttercups dance, looking quite keen!

The onions get spicy, with pizzazz so bright,
While the potatoes just roll, in their comfy delight.
They laugh in the breeze, with the daisies in tow,
Contemplating life as they wiggle and flow.

Calligraphy of the Cattails

Cattails stand tall, with a wink and a nod,
Ink on the marsh, like a pen of a god.
With each stroke of wind, they're writing their song,
The frogs join in chorus, where they all belong.

A heron looks on, with a head held quite high,
Mimicking reeds with a well practiced sigh.
But with a quick flap, he stirs up a scene,
As the cattails just chuckle, keeping things green!

The Whistle of Willow Wands

In the breeze, the willows sway,
Whistles echo, come what may.
Rabbits dance, their ears so tall,
Chasing shadows, having a ball.

Squirrels jest and juggle nuts,
While doves wear little boots and cuts.
Laughter bubbles all around,
As frogs hop high without a sound.

The leaves clap hands, they're quite the crowd,
In sunny patches, they sing loud.
A tale of whimsy, spun from green,
In nature's theater, what a scene!

So if you stroll past this fine spot,
Join the fun, expect a lot.
Beneath the laughter, take your stand,
With willow wands, hold nature's hand.

Euphony in the Eden

In Eden's hug, where giggles bloom,
A snickered breeze sweeps past the gloom.
Birds in bowler hats chirp a tune,
While daisies dance beneath the moon.

A hedgehog tells a knock-knock joke,
As mushrooms giggle, what a cloak!
The roses blush, they blush and beam,
At all the merry, silly dreams.

The sun winks down, a golden jest,
In nature's hug, we're truly blessed.
With laughter ringing, hearts feel light,
Eden's echo sings through the night.

So come and prance, or jump and spin,
In this wild garden, let life begin.
Among the greens, join the jubilee,
Where euphony drapes, we are all free.

The Refrain of the Roots

Deep down low, where secrets hide,
The roots gossip, side by side.
Whispering tales of silly sights,
Under the ground, they share delights.

A worm with specs, so wise and spry,
Winks at ants bustling by.
The roots chuckle, they jest and play,
While crickets sing through night and day.

Mice in capes, they swoop and soar,
Joining the fun, they ask for more.
With every tick-tock of the clock,
The roots unite and start to rock.

So listen close, join in the cheer,
The whispers rise, oh do you hear?
With every grin, and every sound,
The refrain of roots spins round and round.

Gospels of the Greenery

In fields of green, where giggles sprout,
The gospels sing without a doubt.
Every twig tells a funny tale,
As trees sway gently in the gale.

Flowers trade puns, each petal bright,
Their orange laughter sparks the night.
A dandelion, with a crown of fluff,
Quips at weeds, 'You're just not tough!'

Butterflies flit with vibrant glee,
In the choir of green, come sing with me.
Tickled by sunlight, grass bows down,
While gophers make a silly frown.

So gather 'round, let nature flow,
With every blossom, laughter grows.
In greenery's grasp, we find our way,
To tuneful joy, come dance and play.

Chants of the Hidden Grove

In the woods, a squirrel pranced,
He wore a hat, with quite a glance.
His tail was fluffy, a crown of fluff,
Proclaimed himself the woodland stuff.

A bunny danced, with tiny hops,
Said, "I'll show you how to flop!"
But tripped on roots and fell in mud,
His fluffy tale, now coated crud.

A raccoon came, with snacks galore,
Claimed he was chef, we begged for more.
He tossed some berries, all in play,
And shouted, "Dinner's on the way!"

The trees then whispered, "What a show!"
Laughter echoed, from high to low.
In hidden groves, where antics thrive,
Nature's jesters come alive.

Verses Beneath the Boughs

Underneath the giant oak,
A wise old turtle cracked a joke.
He said, "Why did the chicken flee?
To dodge a dance-off, like me!"

The bird just chuckled, perched above,
Said, "My rhythm's what I love!"
They twirled and spun, in silly bliss,
In the shady space, they found their miss.

A fox then joined, with prancing feet,
Declared, "I too can bust a beat!"
But tripped on roots, fell with a flair,
"Next time, I'll practice with more care!"

Laughter rang through branches tall,
Echoing softly, a woodland call.
Down there beneath the leafy shroud,
Even the quiet felt quite loud.

Lullabies of the Bramble

In a bramble, soft and sweet,
A hedgehog hummed, on tiny feet.
He crooned to stars, as night drew near,
"Join my party, bring some cheer!"

A hedgehog's tune, with quirky sound,
Called to creatures all around.
A badger joined, with snore and yawn,
Said, "Can I nap till light of dawn?"

The fireflies twinkled, danced in air,
"Sleep's overrated, you must share!"
So they spun tales of food and fun,
Till moonlit laughter reigned as one.

In brambles dark, the night was bright,
With funny songs, and pure delight.
These woodland creatures found their way,
To sing and dance, 'til break of day.

Songs from the Woodland Floor

On the woodland floor, where laughter blooms,
A skunk showed us his dance micro-glooms.
He slid and kicked, oh what a sight,
And squealed, "You'll see my moves ignite!"

An owl hooted, perched up high,
"Your rhythm's off, and I just sigh."
But when he tried to join the show,
He twisted wrong, making quite a blow.

Across the leaves, the raccoon twirled,
With jars of snacks, his dance unfurled.
He juggled berries, lost one here,
"It's part of the fun, do not fear!"

The wind just chuckled, swayed along,
While all of nature sang their song.
In the glee beneath the leafy lore,
The woodland floor laughed evermore.

Whimsical Whispers of Wood

In the forest, trees begin to sway,
Their branches dance, come out to play.
Leaves chuckle softly, a rustling sound,
As critters hop and twirl around.

Bugs hum tunes as they buzz by,
Worms join in with a slippery sigh.
The sun peeks through, a golden grin,
Nature's laughter starts to spin.

Squirrels chatter with acorn glee,
A jolly troupe beneath a tree.
While daisies giggle in the breeze,
They spread their cheer with such great ease.

Oh, what joy in the greenery found,
With every rustle, a cheerful sound.
As shadows dance, the day goes on,
In this woodland world, we sing along!

Resounding Rhyme of Roots

Beneath the soil, there's much ado,
Roots recite their rhymes anew.
They swap sweet secrets, twirling round,
In underground circles, silly sounds.

Tiny critters lend an ear,
To tales of fungi, far and near.
With each new verse, the laughter spreads,
As snails bet on who wins in beds.

Little pebbles tap a beat,
While gophers join with tiny feet.
For every giggle, the soil will shake,
As nature weaves a joke to make.

Up above, the breezes sigh,
With every chuckle from earth to sky.
In playful tones, they hum and croon,
You'll hear their songs beneath the moon!

Crescendo of Creep

A creeping vine begins to tease,
With every twist, it aims to please.
It tickles walls and climbs up high,
While insects join for a fun-filled sky.

With leafy hands, they swing around,
Spreading cheer all over town.
A funny dance, a twisty game,
As all the greens declare their fame.

Bouncing berries share a laugh,
While mossy carpets craft the path.
The giggling vines begin to bend,
Their joyful curves just seem to blend.

Nature's choir sings in delight,
As it creeps softly into the night.
Every shadow plays a tune,
A merry group beneath the moon!

The Song of the Solstice Shrubs

At solstice time, the bushes sway,
They gather round for a festive play.
With chubby cheeks and twinkling eyes,
They share their jokes beneath the skies.

The elderberry sings a tale,
While neighboring shrubs join in, set sail.
Their leaves flapping, a show of glee,
As laughter rings from tree to tree.

Hedgehogs roll and do a spin,
Their prickly coats a cheerful win.
With every rustle, the fun expands,
As laughter echoes across the lands.

So raise a toast to every shrub,
For in their heart, they form a club.
Beneath the stars, they dance and twirl,
In nature's song, the joy unfurls!

The Ballad of the Blossoms

In the garden, blooms so bright,
Petals dance in sheer delight.
Bees are buzzing, quite a show,
Wearing pollen hats, you know!

Daffodils wear silly hats,
Tickled by the chubby cats.
Sunflowers tilt with cheeky grins,
Waving at the passing winds.

Tulips laugh with colors bold,
Sharing secrets, stories told.
Glancing at the weeds nearby,
"Why so grumpy?" They all sigh!

Laughter echoes through the green,
Nature's joke, the funniest scene.
In the patch, a garden play,
Where every flower steals the day.

Frolics of the Foliage

Leaves do tango in the breeze,
Whispering giggles through the trees.
Sassy branches swing and sway,
Chasing shadows in the fray.

Vines perform a twisty spin,
Tickled by a soft, warm wind.
Frogs in hats—quite the sight,
Leap around with sheer delight!

Mossy carpets carpet bomb,
Dancing squirrels are the charm.
Laughter echoes, rustling cheer,
Nature's party, all are near!

Every leaf a joker plays,
In this green, ridiculous maze.
Foliage frolics never cease,
Each twist and turn, a joy release.

Odes to the Overgrowth

Among the shrubs, a hearty laugh,
Hidden gnomes with witty craft.
Whimsical critters prance about,
What a scene, a lively clout!

Brambles boast of huckleberry,
Sassy nettles, quite the merry.
"Catch us if you can!" they shout,
As the butterflies whirl about.

A bush sings low, a gentle tune,
While dandelions chase the moon.
Wobbly weeds have taken flight,
In this jungle, pure delight!

Amidst the green, the fun unfolds,
Overgrown stories to be told.
Nature knows how to have fun,
In this jungle, laughter runs.

Tones of the Tangle

Twisting vines, a playful game,
Whispering secrets, none to blame.
Tangled stories, quite absurd,
Nature's giggles softly heard.

Berries chuckle, ripe and round,
While squirrels pirouette around.
"Who's a berry?" asks a thrush,
As a hedgehog starts to blush.

Wildflowers boast of colors bright,
Winking at the fading light.
In the chaos, laughter grows,
In every tangle, humor flows.

Jumbles of green, a comical scene,
Where every plant's a merry machine.
In tangled hues, the fun's begun,
Nature's laughter, second to none.

Rustic Riffs of the Rambler

In the garden where gnomes play,
The bushes chat through the day.
A squirrel's got quite the tale,
Of acorns that just can't fail.

The roses giggle in the breeze,
While daisies do as they please.
A lawn mower makes a loud song,
And all the weeds just sing along.

A hedgehog wore a hat askew,
Claiming he was champion too.
The crickets chirp with delight,
As shadows dance into the night.

With laughter under the sun's glow,
These plants put on quite the show.
Each branch and stem helps together,
For fun feels light as a feather.

Fables of Flora

In a thicket thick with tales,
A daisy swayed, telling scales.
"Have you heard of the sage so wise?
He swears he talks to fireflies!"

The lilacs laughed, their petals curled,
As the daisies twirled and twirled.
"Old oak!" cried the vine in glee,
"Do you think you could climb a tree?"

Butterflies joined the raucous cheer,
Wings flapping up the atmosphere.
While ferns with fronds all in a bristle,
Shook with laughter, creating a whistled fizzle.

In a kingdom where ivy romps,
With every thorn, there comes a chomp.
These may be plants with roots so deep,
But they hold secrets we must keep.

The Narrative of New Growth

From a bud came a rumor most bright,
A sprout declared it would take flight.
The carrots whispered, "Stay below!"
While the zinnias put on a show.

"Watch the houseplant," said the fern,
"Growing up, waiting for its turn.
Does it dream of reaching the sky?
Or just want a new pot to try?"

Each cactus claimed it was quite tough,
"Spiky is chic!" said one, laughing rough.
But marigolds grinned, full of cheer,
"Soft petals can conquer all fear!"

So in this garden of mischief and play,
Growth was a party, come what may.
All plants unite for a joyful day,
With roots in the ground, come out and sway!

Poetic Fragments in Ferns

Ferns whisper secrets of the night,
While fireflies share their twinkling light.
"Have you heard," said the leafy bunch,
"About the moth that loves to crunch?"

The thorns were sharp with salty wit,
Concocting tales of pests that hit.
"Did you see that bug in a tussle?
Thought it could flex, but got a bustled."

Petals danced as the breeze blew by,
Tickled pink, they touched the sky.
With laughter woven in green threads,
Even the weeds got out of their beds.

So here's to the jests in earthbound halls,
Where greenery sings and merrily sprawls.
In nature's chaos, we find our song,
Together, the weird and wonderful belong.

Rhythms in the Roots

In the garden, ants parade,
With tiny hats and grand charades.
They stomp and dance on rich brown earth,
Celebrating life, as if it's worth.

A worm joins in, his moves quite slick,
He wobbles and writhes, a clever trick.
While beetles cheer, their shells all shiny,
In this patch, the mood is quite briny.

A sunflower leans, gives a loud cheer,
Singing out tunes for all to hear.
Honeybees buzz, in perfect time,
Creating sweet verses that softly rhyme.

So join the fun, don't stay aloof,
In the foliage, we find our groove.
With roots that wiggle and branches that sway,
Nature's laughter fills the day.

Nature's Secret Chorus

Underneath the leafy shade,
Little critters come out to play.
Squirrels chatter with tails afluff,
In the underbrush, all's just enough.

A crow croaks out a silly tune,
While frogs croak back, a ribbit boon.
The rhythm builds with every croak,
As flowers sway and laughter's woke.

Hummingbirds flit, a blur of bright,
Dancing nectar, a sweet delight.
They twist and twirl, no fear of fall,
In this open air, they heed the call.

Join the throng, don your best smile,
Nature's chorus goes on for miles.
With rustling leaves and chirps all day,
In this wild band, come out and play.

The Lyrics of Lichen

On the rock, lichen spreads its cheer,
Changing colors throughout the year.
With tiny voices, they start a chat,
About the weather, and where they sat.

Moss joins in, with a soft-spoken tune,
Befriending stones like an old monsoon.
The verses rise with an earthy flair,
As fungi giggle, having no care.

A squirrel perks at the wild serenade,
And taps his foot, on the parade.
With every line, the humor grows,
In this mossy saga, the laughter flows.

So listen close, hear the green refrain,
As nature sings, we skip the mundane.
The stage is set, the audience roams,
In this jovial world, we find our homes.

Crescendos of the Canopy

Beneath the branches, shadows play,
Leaves shimmy wildly in disarray.
A chipmunk spins in a dizzy trail,
Trying to tell the tallest tale.

An owl looks down, with eyes so wide,
Wonders what's causing this joyous ride.
Squirrels are laughing, chasing the breeze,
In this green theater, with carefree ease.

A thundercloud puffs and gives a shout,
But the trees just sway and dance without doubt.
The raindrops join with a splashy laugh,
In this woodsy park, they've found their path.

So come, bring joy, do not hold back,
Celebrate the wild, let laughter stack.
For in the canopy's whimsy embrace,
Every moment is a merry chase.

The Chant of the Choking Vines

In the corner sneaks a vine,
Wiggling like it lost a dime.
It chokes the fence with such a grin,
As if it just committed a sin.

A daisy blushes, can't believe,
The vine's antics, oh, deceive!
It twirls and sways in sheer delight,
Making squirrels giggle at the sight.

But when the gardener comes on near,
The vine just shivers, filled with fear.
It holds its breath, all hushed and sly,
Pretending 'round the weeds to lie.

Oh, what a dance, this leafy jest,
The vine thinks it's truly the best!
With every twist, it steals the show,
A cheeky actor in nature's glow.

Phrases of the Petals

Petals whisper with a twirl,
In colors bright that make us hurl.
They giggle in the summer air,
Tickled pink, no signs of care.

A rose with thorns, oh what a tease,
Mimicking the giggles of the bees.
Each bloom a laugh, a silly song,
In the garden where they all belong.

The daisies chat with tulips bold,
Revealing secrets yet untold.
They gossip softly through the breeze,
Feeling quite like playful peas.

With every sway and gentle lift,
They share their joy, a blooming gift.
Nature's jesters, bright and free,
Only to laugh atop the tree.

The Symphony of Shade

Under the leaves, the shadows play,
In the coolness, they dance and sway.
A chorus formed of rustling sounds,
Where cobwebs weave and sunlight bounds.

The tree trunk's bass, a thumping beat,
While squirrels chirp in rhythmic feat.
A melody of nature's cheer,
Composed by every furry peer.

With wiggles and giggles, all around,
The symphony is joy unbound.
Laughter echoes through the day,
In the shadowed spots where critters play.

Oh, listen close, the whispers say,
To the lighthearted tune they lay.
A concert that never has end,
In every nook, where shadows blend.

Notes from the Nutmeg

Nutmeg dreams in cozy shells,
Swaying slow with secret spells.
Spice-laden jokes, they float about,
Making the chefs giggle and shout.

Oh, what fun, this fragrant plot,
As flavors dance in bubbling pot.
The nutmeg's laughter fills the air,
Inviting all to share and care.

In the pantry, it takes a bow,
With cinnamon, it whispers, "Wow!"
Together they stir, what a sight,
Creating dishes, pure delight.

From cookies soft to stews divine,
These notes of joy let hearts align.
In every bite, a sprinkle of cheer,
Nutmeg's orchestra, loud and clear.

Chants of the Hidden Dell

In the shadows where the jests begin,
A squirrel starts a dance, oh what a win!
With acorns as maracas, it sways with glee,
While buzzing bees join in, oh can't you see?

A rabbit plays the lute, quite off the beat,
While devil-may-care, a hedgehog taps its feet.
The grasses wave like hands in the air,
As critters in the dell spread laughs everywhere.

A deer in a top hat hands out the cheese,
While owls take notes sipping on sweet teas.
With giggles and chuckles, the bushes do sway,
As the concert rolls on, till the end of the day.

So if you wander where the wild things play,
Listen for laughter and dance on the hay.
For in this hidden dell where all's bright and swell,
The melodies of nature ring like a spell.

The Arboreal Melodist

Within the branches sings a cheeky thrush,
Each note a tickle, a whimsical push.
The trees start to giggle and sway to the tune,
While foxes dance under a generous moon.

A crow with a trumpet joins in the spree,
Flapping his wings, oh so full of glee.
The owls hold the beat, with their wise old hoots,
While raccoons in tuxedos start jamming with flutes.

Laughter echoes through the boughs and the leaves,
Each rustling whisper makes the woodland breathe.
The wind catches softly the giggling air,
As branches shake out their carefree hair.

So if you find yourself in this lively show,
Join the jovial throng, let your laughter flow.
For in the forest where trees hold the sway,
The arboreal musician will brighten your day.

Soliloquy in the Shrubland

A little fox in the bushes starts to muse,
On the best dance moves he could ever choose.
With a flick of the tail and a wag of the ear,
He giggles aloud, 'Oh, I'll show them cheer!'

A family of badgers break into a jig,
While a hedgehog nearby strums on a twig.
With thorns for a guitar and blooms for a hat,
They poke fun at each other while having a chat.

A chipmunk chimes in with a quick little quip,
"Why did the caterpillar take a long trip?"
"Because it wanted to be a butterfly, you see!
But got stuck in the shrubbery, totally free!"

So in this land where the laughter compiles,
Each tumble, each fall, brings a hundred bright smiles.
The bushland alive with quirky refrains,
In a soliloquy where joy never wanes.

Vibrations of Verdant Essence

In the garden of giggles, the flowers all sway,
As bumblebees boast in their exuberant play.
With pollen as snowflakes, they throw up their wings,
While caterpillars munch on their leafy things.

A parrot recites riddles; oh what a treat!
"Why did the tomato blush? It's just too sweet!"
The daisies all chuckle, the roses turn red,
As rabbits hop by, shaking their heads.

In this verdant realm, where the sun shines bright,
Laughter bubbles up from morning till night.
With squirrels chuckling at antics unknown,
The essence of mirth makes the garden their home.

So join in the tones of this green melody,
Where every small creature sets the spirit free.
For in the vibrations where joy is the quest,
A festival reigns, and humor is blessed.

Fables of the Fronds

In the garden, sneaky thieves,
Steal my herbs, just like leaves.
Dancing weeds in springtime air,
Chasing gnomes without a care.

Frogs in boots jump to the beat,
Grasshoppers tap with tiny feet.
Snails on skateboards zoom around,
Making music, what a sound!

Bumblebees with disco flair,
Buzzing tunes while in mid-air.
Petunias laugh, with petals wide,
As squirrels join the merry ride.

So join the fun, don't delay,
In our leafy cabaret.
With laughter sprouting from each sprig,
Come dance with us, let's dig dig dig!

The Arbor's Anthem

Watch the branches sway and shake,
While the squirrels plot a prank to make.
The oak tree winks, it's seen it all,
As the woodpecker starts to call.

Chirpy finches form a band,
With acorns rolling off the land.
Rabbits hop in fancy shoes,
While daisies giggle, what a ruse!

Underneath the shady boughs,
The silly critters make their vows.
To laugh and sing till stars appear,
In the moonlight, we have no fear.

So join our choir of croaks and coos,
In the arboreal, funny blues.
Let laughter echo through the trees,
As we celebrate with joyful ease!

Mossy Melodies

Mossy carpets make a stage,
Where the ants create a page.
Plucky snails with shells so bright,
Bring the crowd a pure delight.

Overhead, a raccoon jests,
While the frogs outshine the rest.
Worms in ties do the cha-cha,
Leafy lilies say "Hoorah!"

With twinkling lights from fireflies,
They dance beneath the starry skies.
Fungi twirl in silly hats,
While the hedgehogs learn acrobats.

So let us sing, with giggles loud,
Join the fun, invite the crowd.
In this mossy, merry scene,
Let's live our lives like a dream!

Hymns from the Hedges

Whispers from the hedges near,
Tell of tales that bring us cheer.
Bushy brows and leafy caps,
Garden critters share their naps.

Hedgehogs strut in fancy coats,
While sparrows sing on make-do boats.
Charming daisies, hats askew,
Clap along, as we join too!

Bees in sunglasses buzz along,
Spreading pollen for our song.
Toadstools bounce with laughter sweet,
As caterpillars tap their feet.

So lift your voice, don't be shy,
In this garden, we'll reach the sky.
With hymns and laughter intertwined,
In our leafy world, you'll find!

Eclogue of the Elder

In a garden bright, where weeds poke out,
Elders gossip, causing quite a rout.
They argue if daisies could wear a hat,
As squirrels nod wisely, "Oh dear, how flat!"

The roses chuckle, their perfume so bold,
"We'd dance in the sun, if we were not old!"
With petals all ruffled, it's too much to bear,
"Let's nap in the shade, with skin like a pear!"

Beneath the great oaks, they giggle and pout,
For rabbits in coats serenade with a shout.
The breeze plays around, like a sneaky old fox,
Spreading their laughter, like seeds from a box.

A worm plays the lute, joining in on the fun,
The thorns are the clowns, 'neath the warm setting sun.
In this merry land, where strange gatherings teem,
The elders delight in this whimsical dream.

Harmonizing with Holly

Oh Holly stood proud, in her fiery red cloak,
With berries like disco balls, making us poke.
"You think you're so cute," said an acorn nearby,
"But you're just a shrub, with no need to vie!"

The critters all chuckled, as they swayed to her tune,
As wind whispered secrets, beneath the bright moon.
Holly winked at a magpie, who twirled with glee,
"Together we'll dance, you and I, just wait and see!"

The ivy crept closer, tripping over its vines,
"Oh Holly, dear friend, we're two perfect lines!
Let's sing of the mischief the grasshoppers weave,
We'll giggle and prance, oh, don't you believe?"

They harmonized loud, while the night settled in,
With laughter and songs, and a little soft spin.
A rogue breeze caressed them, they twirled to the stars,
In their jolly banter, there's music in jars!

Stanzas of the Shrubland

In the cheerful shrubland, where laughter is free,
A partridge recites poetry under a tree.
The bushes all rustle, in humor they thrive,
While bees tell tall tales, trying to survive.

A prickly old bramble, with wisdom to share,
Tells jokes about thorns that hang in the air.
"Ever heard of the snapdragons, quite often they sneeze?"
With petal-shaped tissues, they brush off the breeze!

A tuft of green grass starts doing a jig,
And mushrooms quite giggly join in, oh so big!
It's a tale of silliness, this leafy refrain,
Where nature's own chorus sings lightly through rain.

As night gently falls, and stars start to peep,
The plants spread their arms, lulling all into sleep.
In their dreamy embrace, lies the joy of the day,
Each shrub wearing smiles, as the moon fades away.

The Tune of Tenacious Thorns

In a kingdom of thorns, where daisies don't dare,
The music plays on, and it dances through air.
With each clever prick, they twang like a string,
Turning grumbles to giggles, oh how they can sing!

A thistle with swagger makes up funny rhymes,
While brambles and thorns plot all their mad crimes.
They jabber and jab, as the buzzards fly by,
"Who knew being thorny could make us so spry?"

They sway to the rhythm of rustling leaves,
Spreading joy like a breeze climbing high in the eaves.
A cast of green characters on a wild romp,
With cackles and chuckles, they formed quite a pomp.

"Let's throw a grand party," a bold rose does shout,
"Bring zest to our thorns, let's twist and spin about!
With laughter our armor, we'll conquer the night,
In this bristly kingdom, let's hold on tight!"

Poetry in the Pasture

In a field of green delight,
Bouncing cows in morning light,
They dance and prance, no care at hand,
Till one trips up and takes a stand.

The sheep all giggle, roll in glee,
As Jamie's stuck in a prickly tree.
The rooster crows, a funny show,
While piglets snort and twist in tow.

Old Farmer Ted, he shakes his head,
'You lot are nuttier than the bread!'
But laughter rings across the land,
With every trip and tumble grand.

So raise a glass to pasture days,
Where giggles burst like summer rays,
In fields where silly creatures roam,
Their playful hearts, forever home.

The Sonnet of Succulents

In pots of clay where prickles sit,
A cactus stands, unbothered, fit,
Its spines like spears in bold array,
Yet somehow charms in a strange way.

The leafy ones, so fat and round,
With smiles that never leave the ground,
They chuckle, 'We need little care,
Just sunlight, love, and some fresh air.'

One day a friend, a curious hare,
Dared to nibble, unaware of the snare,
With one sharp poke, it jumped so high,
Leaving all other plants to cry.

Now cacti wear their tales with pride,
Of bunnies' blunders when they collide,
In pots they dance, a jolly band,
In the sunny light of life so grand.

Ode to Oaken Shadows

Beneath the boughs where squirrels play,
An acorn drops, oh what a day!
A plump young squirrel, spry and spry,
Lands on his tail, and oh my, oh my!

The shade is cool, the breeze is light,
A shadow feels like pure delight,
But when the wind takes branches low,
The critters scatter, dance, and go.

In laughter rings the tree's old song,
Of bumping heads and where they throng,
A band of nutty friends akin,
In leafy laughter, life begins.

So raise a cheer for oaken glades,
Where nature's jesters serenade,
In every rustle, every sound,
The echo of their joy is found.

Hymn of Hushed Histories

In ancient woods, a whisper flows,
Of stories wrapped in leafy prose,
The trees conspire, they plot and scheme,
With roots entwined in funny dream.

A squirrel found a treasure chest,
Filled with nuts, it thought it best,
Yet when it opened, to dismay,
A funny hat rolled out to play.

The owls, wise with laughter strained,
Unraveled secrets, humor gained,
They crackled tales of days gone by,
Where mishaps made the branches sigh.

So sing we now of historical glee,
In woodlands deep where all are free,
With every chuckle, history thrives,
In laughter's echo, nature's jives.

The Wistful Brushstroke

In the garden, colors sway,
A little brush of green and gray,
Painted leaves with giggles twirl,
As bumblebees in chorus whirl.

A daisy tried to sing a tune,
But ended up just howling at the moon,
With petals flapping in a dance,
They plotted for a flower trance.

The tulips gossip, petals tight,
Quarreling about the sunlit light,
While roses write their love letters,
To bees swarming like trendsetters.

So cheer the shrubs, they dance and prance,
With every breezy botanical chance,
In this amusing garden spree,
Nature's jesters, wild and free!

Humming in the Hedges

In the thicket, laughter grows,
With every thump that nature shows,
A rabbit with a silly hat,
Plays hide and seek with a sleepy cat.

Jasmine hums some jazzy beats,
While daisies shuffle their dainty feet,
The hedges giggle, soft and spry,
As butterflies take off and fly.

The crickets clink their tiny cups,
While snail bands tune their slow-up-ups,
With leafy trumpets, they declare,
A concert in the garden air!

Hedges chorus, loud and proud,
With every silly, jovial crowd,
So let the nature giggles ring,
For every shrub is born to sing!

The Amorous Grove

In the grove, where sparrows flirt,
Trees whisper secrets, soft and curt,
With branches swaying to a tune,
While flowers wink beneath the moon.

The violets blush, a shy romance,
While squirrels plot their nutty dance,
With every heart that skips a beat,
The grove becomes a joyful treat.

Lilies laugh in fragrant jest,
Chasing butterflies, it's all a fest,
And mossy carpets, emerald green,
Lay waiting for a dance unseen.

So twirl with blossoms, take a chance,
In this playful, leafy dance,
For love is found in every breeze,
In this grove, beneath the trees!

Fragments of Flora's Voice

In the meadow, whispers soar,
Where flower children laugh and explore,
With petals fluttering in the sun,
A patchwork quilt of joy and fun.

Daffodils trumpet, loud and bright,
With a hint of mischief, just right,
While ivy climbs with clever tact,
Plotting stories, never lack.

The sunflowers, standing tall and proud,
Wave greetings to the passing crowd,
With every rustle in the breeze,
Fragments of giggles dance with ease.

So join the symphony today,
Where flora sings and hums away,
In a chorus of color and cheer,
Nature's laughter, crystal clear!

Ballad of the Wildflower Breeze

A dandelion danced with glee,
While bees played a buzzing symphony.
Lilies joined in, bright and spry,
Tickling each passerby.

The tulips laughed in a cheerful rhyme,
Whispering secrets of summer's prime.
As butterflies flit with flair,
Spreading joy in the fragrant air.

The grass sat, tickled and shy,
Watching the fun as the petals fly.
With every rustle, a secret jest,
Nature's humor at its best.

In this patch of earth so wide,
Jokes bloom where colors collide.
A riot of giggles on the breeze,
Where wildflowers dance with ease.

Lullabies in the Garden Shade

Under the branches, soft and low,
The flowers hum a gentle show.
With every sway, a playful tune,
As crickets chirp beneath the moon.

A timid fern gives a shy sigh,
While daisies wink as they pass by.
The violets giggle in secret glee,
Sharing tales of the buzzing bee.

Leaves rustle like a lullaby,
Softly sung where the shadows lie.
A serenade of silly sighs,
Passed between the fluttering flies.

The garden whispers, hushed and bright,
Under the stars, delight takes flight.
With every breeze, a quirky blend,
In the garden where giggles mend.

The Bushes' Secret Tune

In the thicket where laughter curls,
The bushes sway, joined in twirls.
Whispers float on the evening air,
As lighthearted shadows dance with flair.

The brambles hum a cheeky song,
With winkles arranged all along.
While hedgehogs scuttle to the beat,
Turning quiet paths into a treat.

A playful breeze stirs soft and quick,
As flowers blush and petals flick.
The bushes play their leafy game,
With nature's jesters claiming fame.

On every branch, a giggly tale,
Where laughter floats like a feathered sail.
In the secret glade, joy's not a rune,
But the bushes' very own sweet tune.

Murmurs Among the Petals

Petals giggle in the warm sunlight,
As soft whispers fill the air tonight.
With bugs that tap dance on the leaves,
Nature plays tricks, oh what mischief weaves!

Chirping crickets invite the show,
While ladybugs say, 'Look at us glow!'
Each flower drops a cheeky pun,
While squirrels sneak, conjuring fun.

In blooms of colors, laughter swells,
With stories that only nature tells.
The scent of mischief wafts about,
Where flowers giggle, there's never doubt.

A riot of hues in every glance,
Sprinkled with sprights that twirl and prance.
In this garden, joy will not stall,
For every petal, there's laughter for all.

Murmurs of the Undergrowth

In the thicket, whispers rise,
Critters laughing, what a prize!
Squirrels chatter, seeds on hold,
Making jokes that never get old.

Beneath the ferns, a secret show,
Grasshoppers dance, putting on a glow.
The mushrooms giggle, hats askew,
While crickets sing a tune so blue.

A hedgehog trips on dewy vine,
"Oh pardon me," he says with a twine.
The bushes sway, they laugh along,
A jolly mix, where all belong.

In tangled roots, a chorus plays,
Tunes of life in sunlight rays.
Oh, what fun in this green land,
Nature's humor, always grand!

Duets of the Dappled Sun

Beneath the leaves, the shadows prance,
Flowers twirl in a merry dance.
A pair of robins takes the stage,
Singing tunes that spark a rage.

Daisies shout, "We're the best!"
While dandelions start the jest.
Bumblebees hum with a zany beat,
Chasing petals; oh, what a feat!

The sun dips low, a golden glow,
Laughter echoes, to and fro.
Each branch joins in with a chime,
Creating tunes that defy time.

So join the mirth, let spirits soar,
In this concert, we'll never bore.
Every leaf a note, every breeze a sigh,
Under the sun, we'll dance and fly!

The Rhapsody of Twigs

A twig in hand begins to play,
A tiny flute, come join the fray!
The frogs croak out a melody,
Bouncing notes from tree to lea.

The winds will hum a silly tune,
While chipmunks join, whoop, and swoon.
Each rustling leaf chimes in with cheer,
A comedy, for all to hear!

Barking dogs bark offbeat now,
As owls hoot giggles, take a bow.
The branches sway, they join the fun,
In this rhapsody of everyone.

From twigs to trunks, a joyful spree,
Nature's orchestra, wild and free.
With every pluck and every pluck,
We laugh along; oh, what luck!

Anthems of the Arborvitae

In leafy homes, the ants have planned,
A circus show, oh, isn't it grand?
With acorns tossed and a daring leap,
Even the snails are making a sweep.

The trees sway gently in their pride,
Hosting creatures here inside.
A raccoon juggles acorns, too,
As laughter echoes, who knew?

The sun sets low for a final act,
The critters cheer, how sweet, how packed!
From roots to tops, they celebrate,
In the grand slam, they're all first-rate!

Each branch a note, each leaf a cheer,
Together united, year after year.
In this green kingdom of wild delight,
The anthems sing into the night!

www.ingramcontent.com/pod-product-compliance
Lightning Source LLC
Chambersburg PA
CBHW071844160426
43209CB00003B/413